A Question of History

★

Did the celts use hair gel?

and other questions about the **STONE, BRONZE** and **IRON AGES**

Tim Cooke

WAYLAND

www.waylandbooks.co.uk

First published in Great Britain in 2021
by Wayland

© Hodder and Stoughton, 2021

Credits:
Editor: Julia Bird
Design and illustrations: Matt Lilly
Cover design: Matt Lilly

ISBN hb 978 1 5263 1540 3
ISBN pb 978 1 5263 1541 0

Printed and bound in China

MIX
Paper from
responsible sources
FSC® C104740

FSC
www.fsc.org

Picture credits:
Alamy: Juan Aunion 20; Sabena Jane Blackbird 5b;
Drew Buckley 30; Mark Dunn 21; Robert Estall 19b; HIP
front cover, 1, 6t, 6cl, 7t, 11, 24; Chris Howes/Wild Places
14b; David Hunter 23; Iconpix 10; Interfoto 8b; Lanmas 25t;
Nearby 15c; Viktor Onyshchenko 20; Maurice Savage 7b;
Skyscan Photolibrary 17.
Shutterstock: Anneka 9; Anita van der Broek 5t; Rob Duncalf
8c; Formatoriginal 25b; Daniele Gay 12t; Guliveris 29; Alan
Kraft 14t; D MacDonald 22; PTZ 4, 12c; Ian Redding 16;
Minakryn Ruslan 15tl; Weha 26; Edward Westmacott 19t.

Wayland
An imprint of
Hachette Children's Group
Part of Hodder and Stoughton
Carmelite House
50 Victoria Embankment
London EC4Y 0DZ

An Hachette UK Company
www.hachette.co.uk
www.hachettechildrens.co.uk

Contents

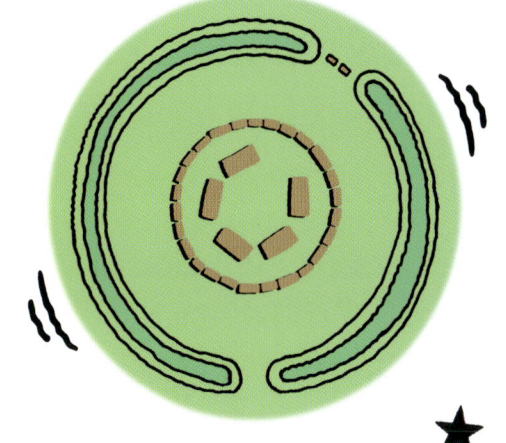

Ancient Britain

When Britain was separated from Europe about 8,000 years ago, the original inhabitants lived in scattered groups all over the island. These Neolithic, or Stone Age, Britons lived in caves and other natural sites.

BYE BYE EUROPE ... FOR NOW ...

European influence

From around 3000 BCE, settlers began to arrive from mainland Europe. Or perhaps ideas from Europe arrived and spread through Britain. Or a mixture of the two. People in Britain started living in small villages, where they farmed for a living and built monuments of earth or stone. Today, one of their monuments is still world famous: **STONEHENGE**.

Archaeologists have been studying Stonehenge for hundreds of years, but they still don't really know why it was built! That's the problem with lots of ancient history. There aren't any records to read – just objects and places from which we try to figure out the past.

VERY NICE. BUT WHAT'S IT FOR?!

Bonkers Bronze Age

By around 2000 BCE, when Stonehenge was completed, the Bronze Age had begun. More new ideas – or perhaps new people – arrived from Europe. People made objects from bronze, such as tools and weapons, and used bell-shaped pottery containers, or beakers (see pages 6–7).

Life on the hill-age

For centuries, the British settled in lowland regions in southern England. From about 800 BCE, they began to build banked enclosures on hills.

These are known as hillforts. They may have protected settlements – but they might just have been huge cattle pens!

MOO KNOWS?

On the record

Is there anything we **DO** know for sure? Yes! By about 750 BCE, the Iron Age had reached Britain. People used iron to make stronger tools and weapons.

Spear head

Celtic arrivals

When the first record of Britain was written down in 325 BCE, by a Greek named Pytheas, the island was already home to many Celts who had come from Europe to settle in Britain. But how many Celts there were, when they arrived and why they had come remain … uncertain.

The best way to find answers is to ask questions – so get ready to turn the page and start asking!

How did Stone Age Britons tell their cups apart?

HEY – THAT'S MY CUP! ISN'T IT?

No one wants to drink from someone else's cup. **YEUCH!** But what if all cups looked the same?

An early Bronze Age beaker

Bell bottoms

In about 2400 BCE, a new sort of cup started turning up in Britain. These were bell beakers – pottery vessels with a slightly bulging bottom, so they looked like upside-down bells. The beakers were decorated by pressing designs or cords into the clay. They also came in slightly different shapes.

So it's probably true to say that no two beakers were alike.

Cup half-full?

The beakers were probably used for drinking. Of course. It was about now that Europeans began brewing barley, so perhaps the beakers were for beer. But they also had other purposes:

- melting ore to make copper
- holding food
- holding the remains of the dead
- use in rituals.

People living in Spain and Portugal probably made the first beakers, and the skill spread through Europe to Britain. Experts in ancient beakers (yes, that IS a job) can use artefacts to date the rough order in which this spread happened. But they can't answer this question:

How did the beakers spread, and who spread them?

HEY – ISN'T THAT MY BUTTON?

Or cup half-empty?

Many archaeologists assumed the beakers were made by a people they named, er, the Beaker Folk, who spread through Europe, displacing the people already there. That's because beakers didn't turn up in new places on their own. They came with a whole 'package' of new stuff, like buttons with V-shaped holes for the threads.

It's in the bones!

Archaeologists have examined DNA in bones from Neolithic Britain. (DNA is the chemical that allows parents to pass on characteristics, such as eye colour, to their children.) The tests suggest a huge migration of newcomers to Britain around 2400 BCE, pushing the earlier inhabitants aside.

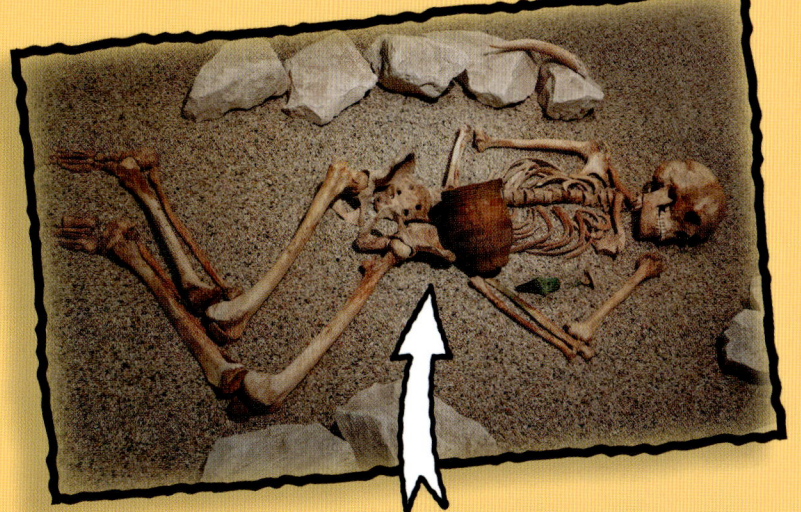

This Bronze Age grave, discovered near Stonehenge, held the skeleton of a man. Analysis of his bones revealed he had grown up near the Alps in Europe. The grave also held bell beakers, copper knives and gold.

Did ancient Britons invent Lego?

Well, the Britons certainly loved building blocks so, in a way, yes. At Stonehenge, the stones were held in place by studs that fitted into holes. Just like … Lego.

Castlerigg Stone Circle in the Lake District, UK, is believed to be between 4,000 and 5,000 years old.

Fun with stones

Stonehenge is the most famous Stone Age monument in Britain, but there are lots of others. In all, there are about 1,300 sites where ancient Britons erected standing stones in circles. In other places, they built tombs called dolmens, which had three or more upright stones with a large 'roof' slab across the top to form an open chamber.

A dolmen in Cornwall, UK

Heavyweight builders

These stone slabs can weigh 80 tonnes – and sometimes double that. If that makes you wonder how ancient builders lifted such huge stones into the air, one theory is that … they didn't.

(1) First, find a good site where your dolmen will be visible. Drag a large stone to the place. Dig a deep hole and pull the stone using ropes so the bottom drops into it.

(2) Then repeat the process to place a second upright stone. Fill up the gap between the stones with earth, and build ramps on either side.

(3) Take your flat top stone and pull it up one of the ramps on rollers made from tree trunks. Lay the stone across the uprights.

(4) Now dig away all the soil, leaving just the stones.

Round and round

Neolithic peoples built stone circles all across Northern Europe – but no one really knows why.

Perhaps they were places for rituals to contact the gods. Or perhaps they were used for burials and other purposes. Some seem to align with the sunrise on special days of the year, so perhaps they were a kind of calendar. No one really knows for sure.

Was the White Horse really a cat?

WHAT'S SO SPECIAL ABOUT HORSES, ANYWAY?

You've probably seen pictures of white horses carved into the British countryside. They're visible from far away. They're white because cutting away the turf exposes the chalk underneath.

(They only occur in places with chalky soil, of course – otherwise they'd be brown horses.)

Horse on the hill

The oldest chalk horse is about 3,000 years old. It gallops across the top of a hillfort at Uffington, in Oxfordshire.

Or perhaps it doesn't.

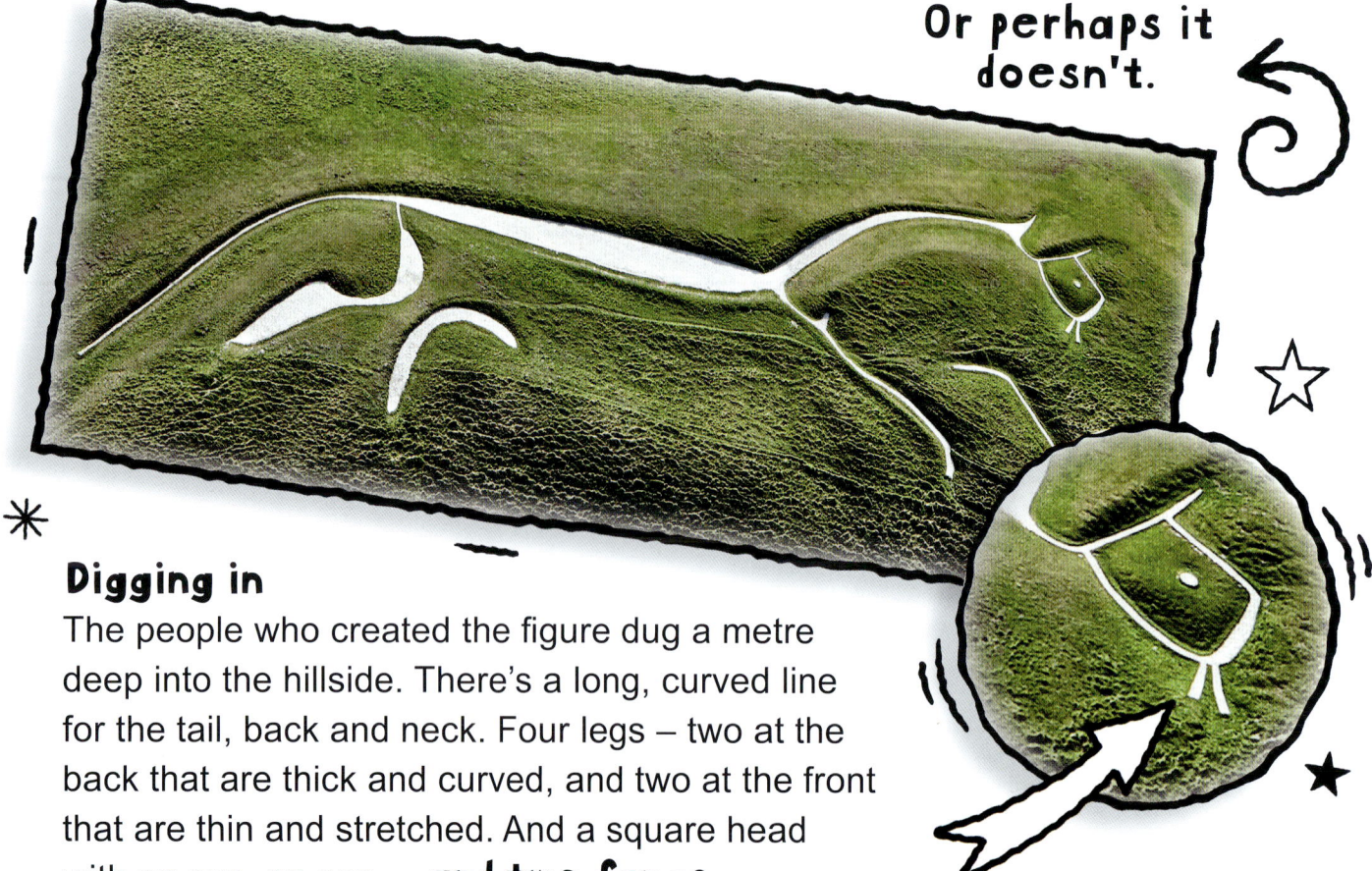

Digging in

The people who created the figure dug a metre deep into the hillside. There's a long, curved line for the tail, back and neck. Four legs – two at the back that are thick and curved, and two at the front that are thin and stretched. And a square head with an eye, an ear … **and two fangs**.

HANG ON!

Hello kitty?

Everyone knows that horses don't have fangs. So even though the White Horse has been called a white horse for over a thousand years, perhaps it's not.

> I'M A PUSSY CAT REALLY!

What else could it be? One suggestion is that it is a sabre-toothed cat. This prehistoric hunter was the size of a lion, with fangs up to 28 cm long.

Scary!

Horse sense

The problem is that sabre-toothed cats were extinct by about 10,000 BCE, long before the White Horse was made. So perhaps it is a horse – but drawn by a rubbish artist.

A similar horse was carved on a bronze container found nearby. So perhaps the horse was a symbol of a local tribe.

Or perhaps it was just a horse.

Riding or pulling?

Horses were important in Iron Age Britain. They even appeared on coins, so they probably had some kind of religious or spiritual meaning. However, we don't know if anyone actually rode them as they were mainly used for pulling carts or war chariots. By the time the Romans invaded in 55 BCE, however, some Britons were definitely riding horses – even into battle.

A gold coin made by the Celtic Catuvellauni tribe, dating from around 10 BCE. It shows a man riding a horse, holding a war trumpet.

Did aliens land at Stonehenge?

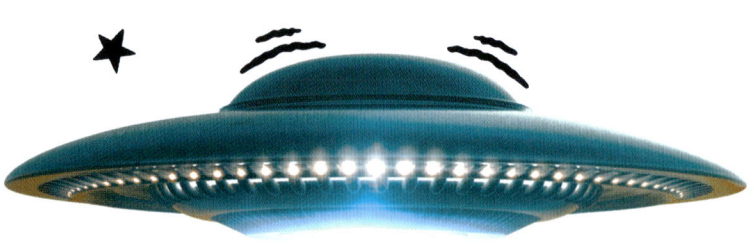

Er, no. Of course not! It's true that some people have suggested that aliens built the stone circles as a landing site for spacecraft. But that's only because you can see them from the air.

Here are some other suggestions for what Stonehenge was used for:

- a meeting place for Druids
- a calendar for farmers
- a computer to predict eclipses
- a ceremonial site for the dead.

Who knows?

Most experts think that Stonehenge is linked to death. Human remains were buried in holes around the outside of the site. And some stones line up with sunrise and sunset on the longest and shortest days of the year. So it might have been a sort of calendar. As for the Druids, they only arrived in Britain 3,000 years after Stonehenge was built.

A leading expert on Stonehenge said this ...

NO ONE WILL EVER HAVE A CLUE WHAT ITS SIGNIFICANCE WAS.

Huh. Not very helpful.

Stage by stage

We do know that Stonehenge was built in stages.
Let's call them I, II and III (because that's what they're called).

Stonehenge I (c. 3100 BCE)

Builders dug a large circular ditch to create an earthwork bank with two entrances. Inside, they dug a ring of holes and filled them in. (Weird.) It was used for about 500 years, then abandoned.

Stonehenge II (c. 2100 BCE)

Builders set up two circles of stone pillars, one inside the other. There were about 80 of these bluestones.

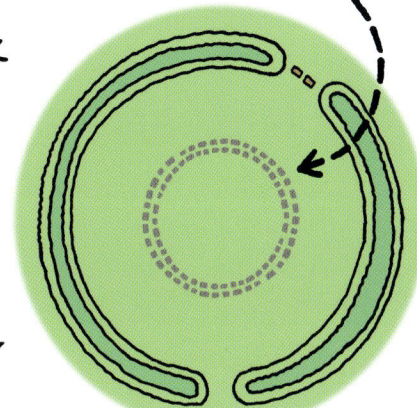

Stonehenge III (c. 2000 BCE)

The builders removed the bluestones and built a ring of huge sarsen stones joined by a horizontal lintel. Inside the ring was a horseshoe of five sarsen arches. Over the next 500 years, the bluestones were put back up in the middle of the monument.

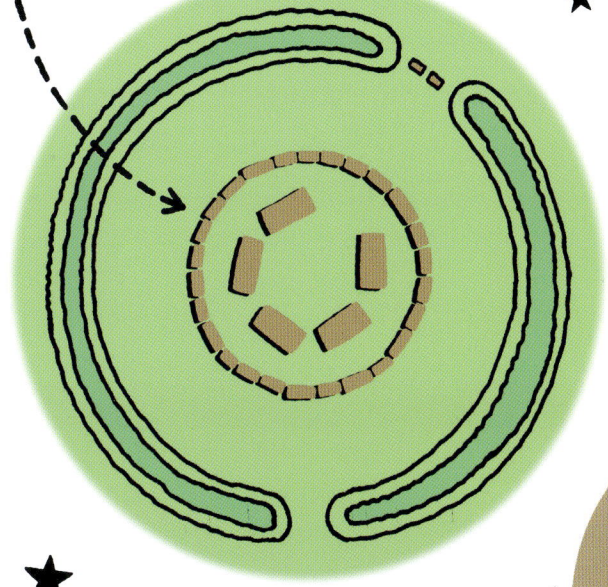

Take your time!

Stonehenge's shape was complete by 2000 BCE, but its design wasn't final until about 1100 BCE – 2,000 years after the first version was begun. The people who built the last version probably didn't even know why Stonehenge was built. And today we still don't know. But we do know it wasn't for aliens.

SO WHERE ARE WE SUPPOSED TO LAND?

What made Great Orme great?

About 4,000 years ago, miners started digging into a rocky headland at Great Orme in North Wales. Within a thousand years, it was full of tunnels that stretched underground for kilometres.

Inside the headland, the tunnels were so small that only children aged about five or six could fit into them. Or hobbits.

Mining

Miners dug the tunnels using hammers made from animal bones and granite stones from the local beach. They burned candles made from animal fat.

Copper bottomed

What was the point of all this effort? **Copper**. The Great Orme was full of tons of a green mineral called malachite. It was used to make jewellery, paint and makeup – but malachite could also be crushed and melted to produce copper.

Malachite

Copper was useful – but it was a bit soft. But from about 2100 BCE, smiths learned to make it even more useful by melting it with a little tin to create bronze.

Bronze Age axe heads

Bronze was:

- harder
- easier to melt and shape
- more resistant to rust.

Bronze was better than stone or copper for making tools and weapons. It bent less easily, and had sharper edges that did not blunt or wear out. British smiths became famous for their skill – and the Great Orme became the largest copper mine in the world.

Far and wide

The tin used to make bronze came from Devon and Cornwall, around 500 km away from Great Orme. Once made, the bronze was traded in Britain and throughout mainland Europe.

New arrivals

Some people believe the early Bronze Age saw the arrival of new immigrants to England from what is now the southern Netherlands and northern Belgium. These people traded across Europe, and buried their dead under huge barrows with rich grave goods. They were probably relatively wealthy – and organised enough to finish the last phases of Stonehenge.

15

Did the Britons love a good view?

FORT ON A HILL, HILL WITH A FORT ... I'VE GOT IT! HILLFORT!

All over southern England the tops of hills have been shaped into rings of walls and ditches looking out over the surrounding countryside. There are about 2,000 of these structures, which some bright spark named hillforts. But are they really?

Well, yes. Maybe. Given that these structures are nearly 3,000 years old, it's hard to know for sure!

Run for the hills!

Some experts think that the Iron Age was a time of frequent warfare, not just in Britain, but everywhere. Groups of farmers fought over the best land, or water for their crops ... or whatever else they needed. In which case, living on fortified hilltops might make sense.

Apart from ... well, some of the forts are pretty rubbish. Many have just a single ditch and wall. At Scratchbury in Wiltshire enemies could look down at the layout of the fort and plan where to attack.

Scratchbury Hillfort

16

Attack us, we dare you!

So if the hillforts weren't forts, what were they? Let's be honest: no one would spend ages moving tons of soil just to create some banks to sit and look out over the view.

The answer may lie in Iron Age ideas about warfare. Experts suggest that some farmers actually tried to avoid conflict. Instead, they tried to intimidate their neighbours by showing off their power, for example by building earthworks that looked strong and powerful.

YOU DON'T WANT TO FIGHT ME – I'VE GOT GREAT BIG ... EARTHWORKS!

 Many hillforts were built near places that already had some kind of spiritual meaning, such as Neolithic burial mounds or barrows – so perhaps the hillforts had some kind of spiritual purpose, too.

A-maze-ing defences

Some hillforts are much better defended than others. At Maiden Castle in Dorset, a series of soil banks around the hill form a maze to prevent attackers reaching the top. There were also rings of wooden walls to protect the hilltop, where the inhabitants lived in wooden homes with straw roofs.

Much better!

Maiden Castle

Did Druids murder with mistletoe?

Here's a bit of advice. If someone in a Druid costume offers you mistletoe, don't eat it. It might cause stomach pains, blurred vision and diarrhoea.
Oh … and possibly death.

That's right.

The little branches and white berries that people kiss under at Christmas are poisonous. But they were also sacred to the Druids, who were some of the most important people in Iron Age Celtic society in Britain.

Druids had a lot of roles:
- political advisors
- legal advisors
- doctors
- priests
- judges.

DELICIOUS PIECE OF MISTLETOE?

ERRR – NO THANKS!

Trust me, I'm a Roman

Most of what we know about the Druids comes from the Romans, who met them when they invaded Britain and other Celtic lands. It's worth remembering that the Romans and the Celts didn't always get along.

So maybe the Romans were a bit, er, BIASED.

Sip, don't gulp!

According to the (not completely neutral) Romans, the Druids harvested mistletoe in the woods. (It's a parasitic plant, by the way, that grows on trees.)

A Druid wearing a white robe climbed the tree and cut it with a curved sickle. Another made sure to catch it before it reached the ground. They made a drink from mistletoe to use in their rites. Even though it was poisonous.

(Let's hope they only sipped it.)

Mistletoe murder

When the 2,000 year-old body of a man was found in a peat bog in Cheshire, he had mistletoe pollen in his stomach. Some people think that means he was given mistletoe to eat before being killed and thrown into the bog as part of a sacrifice. Others think some mistletoe pollen might just have blown onto his lunch while he was eating under a tree.

Mistletoe

You're no Druid!

Every Midsummer's Day, people welcome the sunrise at Stonehenge wearing white robes and calling themselves Druids. Er, what?

We've already seen that the ancient Druids had nothing to do with Stonehenge. And the modern version of Druidism only began in the 1800s, when people got a bit romantic about the ancient past and made up a religion based on what they thought the Celts believed (wrongly, it turns out).

How did a hard ard change Britain?

IT'S 'ARD TO FARM WITHOUT THEM!

Your first question is probably, 'What on Earth is an ard?!' An ard was a type of plough, used for farming. Ploughs were very important in ancient Britain.

Ard

Grinding grains

Britons living in villages usually worked on the nearby land. They grew grains such as wheat and barley, which they ground into flour on a stone called a **quern**.

Full-on flour

Flour is really versatile. You can use it to make:

- bread
- porridge
- beer.

That was great, because the main items in the Iron Age diet were:

- bread
- porridge
- beer.

People also caught fish and birds for food, or hunted game such as deer. They probably also gathered berries, leaves and nuts.

Ploughing ahead

The Iron Age began in Britain in about 800 BCE. Iron was harder than bronze, so iron weapons and tools were stronger.

THIS IS MUCH BETTER!

The problem with the ard was that it wasn't very hard. Whoops! Its wooden tip often broke or failed to turn rocky soil. Replacing it with an iron tip meant that farmers could plough areas with rougher soil. That meant they could plant more crops and harvest more grain.

Changing society

Once farmers had enough food for themselves, they could exchange the rest for other things they needed or sell it. With more food available, more people could stop farming, live in towns and work as craftspeople or merchants.

Which slowly began to change the whole of society.

Later in the Iron Age, craftspeople produced beautifully decorated shields such as this one, dating from around 350–50 BCE.

✳ Animal farm ✳

Most people didn't eat much meat, but farmers raised cattle, sheep and pigs. They were useful for their meat, milk and skins. Their poo made good manure for crops. And cows could also help pull ards.

Did Iron Age Britons wear wellies?

Well no, they didn't actually have wellies. Or rubber. Rubber trees are native to the American rainforests, not to the British Isles. Rubber only appeared here in the 1700s – and that was as erasers, not as boots.

Rainy days

But the climate during the Iron Age **WAS** pretty wet and cool. There were many lakes and ponds, and some Britons built their homes in the middle of bodies of water. These crannogs (as they were known) were particularly popular in Ireland and Scotland.

THESE ARE AMAZING! WHAT DO YOU MEAN THEY HAVEN'T BEEN INVENTED YET?!

An island of calm

Crannogs were artificial islands of stone or branches held together with timber uprights. They were used to build roundhouses that were accessible only by canoe or coracle (a small boat shaped like a bowl).

YOU CAN'T KEEP US OUT!

Crannogs were easy to defend – except against ducks!

Round and round

Most Britons didn't live on the water. They lived in villages in circular houses (or roundhouses) that were often built close together and enclosed by earthen or wooden walls. The houses had a low wall made of wattle and daub, with a tall conical roof made of thatch resting on a frame of timber.

A reconstructed Iron Age village in Pembrokeshire in Wales

Happy home, happy hearth

Inside a roundhouse was an open hearth. A fire burned there around the clock. Woe betide anyone who let it go out!

The fire was used for cooking and to give heat and light. There were clay cooking pots and a large bronze cauldron might have hung from a frame over the fire. Smoke rose up into the roof and escaped through the thatch.

Storing food

One of the biggest challenges in the Iron Age was stopping food from going rotten. That way it could last through the winter. People hung fish, meat and herbs in the roofs of their homes, so they would dry in the fire smoke and be preserved. They buried grain in deep, bell-shaped pits dug into the ground or stored it in granaries that were raised off the ground to keep out rats and mice.

Did the Celts use hair gel?

The Romans invaded Britain in 43 CE.
If one thing shocked them about the Celts more
than anything else, it was probably the Celts' hair!

> **WHAT'S GOING ON WITH HIS HAIR?!**

Hair-raising!

The Romans claimed that the Celts used lime or chalk to colour their hair blonde. Not only that, they also used a kind of gel that made their hair stiff, so they could shape it into spikes.

They probably thought it looked good. It might also have helped them look a bit taller and more scary to their enemies.

A popular style was to tie the hair back in a ponytail. Or to pile it up on top of the head in a big knot.

Colourful clothes

Celtic clothes were brightly coloured using dye from berries and plants. Women and girls spun sheep's wool into yarn that they wove into cloth on upright looms in their roundhouses.

Top trousers

Another thing that surprised the Romans was something we all take for granted today: trousers. For the Romans, who still wore togas and tunics, the leg coverings men wore under their tunics were very unusual. Not so much Celtic women, whose long woollen dresses were covered by shawls held in place by brooches or pins. Decorated, of course.

Because the Celts loved ～ BLING. ～

They wore jewellery whenever they could, including gold, silver or copper pendants, bracelets, brooches and torcs. Eh, what? Torcs were stiff rings of metal worn around the neck. But only if you were important.

The Celts loved to wear a pattern called plaid (tartan to you and me).

Talking torcs

Torc

The best and most valuable torcs were made of gold and intricately decorated. But only if you were VERY important. Torcs were worn by the best Celtic warriors, but also by other important men and women. They were so valuable they were buried with the dead. Torcs might also have been sacrificed to the gods by being thrown into lakes or bogs.

Did Celtic warriors really paint themselves blue?

BATTLE ON, SHIRT OFF!

Most people going into battle against enemies carrying swords and spears would put on armour. Or at least their thickest clothes. Not the Celts. According to the Romans, they took their clothes OFF.

Bare battles

Ancient Roman historians left accounts of how Celtic warriors went into battle naked. One said they were worried about their clothes catching on brambles as they ran.

You'd think they'd also be worried about other things catching on brambles!

Woad

Lend me your ears

Roman general Julius Caesar, who landed in Britain in 55 BCE, noted in horror that the Celts generally wore very little – unless it was really, really cold. He also wrote that the Celts painted themselves blue, possibly using a plant called **WOAD**.

The idea of terrifying naked blue warriors running into battle soon spread.

Are you bonkers?

We know that some Celts wore chain-mail shirts and leather armour, so the stories about fighting naked probably only applied to small groups of warriors who were either:

1. too poor to afford armour (or clothes);
2. or mad.

The second group, called the Gaesatae, fought the Romans in Europe rather than in Britain. They were fanatical warriors, and terrifying to meet on the battlefield. However, their lack of protection meant that in fact the Romans usually defeated them quite easily. Which makes sense when you think about it.

Because they were starkers and the Romans had armour.

Telling tales

The Romans spread stories about the Celts being naked and a bit mad. Why? Because the story reminded people back home that Rome's enemies were such savages that they didn't even wear clothes!

Describing the Celts as being fierce (and a bit mad) also made the point that the Roman army that defeated them, and eventually took conrol of Britain, was even fiercer.

This Roman statue shows a (naked) Celtic warrior dying from his battle wounds.

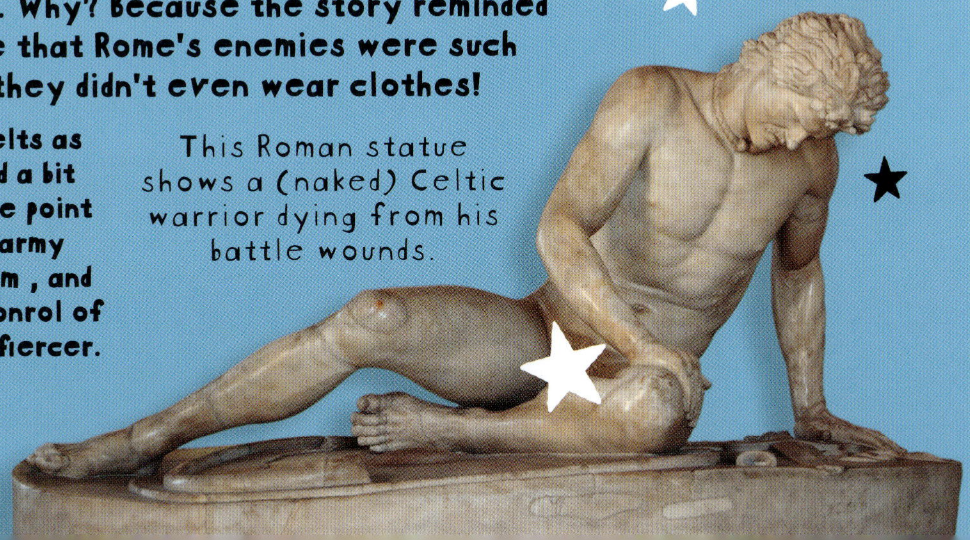

Quick-fire questions

Why did the Britons drag heavy stones so far?

The bluestones at Stonehenge could only come from one place: the hills near Preseli in Wales. That was 225 km away. The builders didn't have wheels or carts, so they probably dragged the heavy stones over the ground on rollers or sleds. But archaeologists don't really know why. Which is … frustrating. One theory is simple. The rocks in Preseli were so easy to cut out from the cliffs in the right shapes for pillars that it made up for the effort of moving them.

YOU CAN'T HAVE MY HEAD!

Why did ancient Britons collect … heads?!

A few sources say that Celtic warriors cut the heads off their enemies. Some say they tied the heads to their horses. Others say they simply kept them. (In fact, most of these stories are about European Celts rather than British Celts.) British Celts seem to have included many images of heads in their artwork and jewellery. Some experts think the Celts believed that the soul lived in the head, which made your enemy's head a source of great spiritual power (especially when it wasn't attached to your enemy).

Did the Celts really worship trees?

In the late Bronze Age, Celts in ancient Britain seem to have worshipped trees. Some had sacred groves, but others worshipped individual trees. And some even worshipped individual trees inside sacred groves. They carried out rituals and made sacrifices there. The Celts probably believed that trees had a religious power because they lived for centuries, they died and were reborn every year and they joined the underworld to the sky. Their favourite trees to worship? The oak, the yew and the ash.

Were the Britons and Celts the same?

Well, kind of, yes. Historians aren't sure who arrived in Britain when. There were ancient Britons living in, er, ancient Britain long before the start of the Iron Age in around 750 BCE. Then Celts arrived, who were related to the Celts of Europe. The Celts lived alongside the Britons, and are often simply called Britons.

Remember it this way: all Celts in Britain were Britons, but not all Britons were Celts!

Glossary

Align To form a straight line with something.

Archeologist Someone who studies physical remains of the past.

Artefact An object made by people.

Barrow A mound of earth built over a grave.

Biased Typically preferring one thing.

Bluestone A type of bluish stone pillar used at Stonehenge.

Eclipse When the Sun and Moon align in the sky.

Enclosure An area of land surrounded by a barrier.

Extinct Having no surviving members of a species.

Grove A group of trees.

Hearth A space on a floor for a fire.

Intimidate To frighten someone into doing something.

Lawspeaker Someone who remembers the laws of a tribe.

Lintel A horizontal stone laid across two upright stones.

Migration The movement of people from one place to another.

Monument A building or structure that has a historical meaning.

Neolithic Belonging to the later part of the Stone Age.

Ore A solid material from which metal can be obtained.

Parasitic Describes something that lives off another living organism.

Rituals Solemn religious ceremonies performed in a set way.

Sacred Believed to be special and holy.

Sacrifice Something valuable that is offered as a gift to the gods.

Sarsen A large boulder of sandstone.

Sickle A tool with a semicircular blade used to cut plants.

Tribe A group of people who live together and share ways of life and traditions.

Wattle and daub A building material made from woven sticks covered in mud.

Bluestones in the hills near Preseli in Wales.

30

Mini timeline

c.3000 BCE
Settlers arrive
in Britain from mainland
Europe.

c.2400 BCE
The Beaker culture
begins in Britain.

c.2000 BCE
Stonehenge is
completed.

c.750 BCE
The Iron Age begins
in Britain.

c.750 BCE
Celts from Europe
reach Britain.

43 BCE
The Romans invade
Britain.

Further reading

Websites

www.bbc.co.uk/bitesize/topics/z82hsbk/articles/zpny34j

This BBC Bitesize page is an introduction to the Stone, Bronze and Iron ages.

www.bbc.co.uk/history/handsonhistory/ancient-britain.shtml

This BBC page has links to many activities related to ancient Britain.

www.english-heritage.org.uk/members-area/kids/prehistoric-england/

This English Heritage site explores ancient sites all over England.

www.theschoolrun.com/homework-help/celts

This site has a list of Top 10 facts about the Celts.

Books

History Detective Investigates: Stone Age to Iron Age
by Claire Hibbert (Wayland, 2016)

Explore! Stone, Bronze and Iron Ages
by Sonya Newland (Wayland, 2017)

Writing History: The Stone Age
by Anita Ganeri (Franklin Watts, 2019)

Time Travel Guides: The Stone Age and Skara Brae
by Ben Hubbard (Franklin Watts, 2020)

Index